Poems from the Edge of Spring

by

Elise Skidmore

Heart Ally Books
Camano Island, Washington

Published by:
Heart Ally Books
26910 92nd Ave NW C5-406, Stanwood, WA 98292
Published on Camano Island, WA, USA
www.heartallybooks.com

ISBN: 978-1-63107-000-6

Dedicated

to my parents, whose love and support was never ending
to my husband, for all the lifetimes of love
and to my daughters, who are my finest legacy

Contents

My Mother's Hands

I find comfort in aloneness
where I can let my thoughts drift
like a discarded love letter
fluttering in the breeze
inhale deep gusts of imperfect memory
or contemplate my hands

I have my mother's hands
their shape, texture, and dexterity
not finely manicured but
working hands
helping hands
loving hands

I hold her hand and we are one
in silent communication
pleading not to let go
reassurance I'm still here
speaking love through
entwined fingers and kissing palms

With my mother's hands
I stroke her face and hair
willing her to know through my touch
that I love her more than she ever loved herself
that her best was good enough
and she deserves so much more than life ever handed her

I find comfort in aloneness
for I am never alone
My mother is always there
in my hands
and in my heart

Down the Highway

Wrapped tight in self-control,
propelled down crowded highways
with scores of duty to untangle,
I silence vague notions
of driving into the sunset
as far as the cash in my pocket will take me,
wondering how far that would be,
and what
would I be
running away from
or forward to.

Too timid to take the steps
to advance or retreat
I stick to the tedious route before me.
Reflected in the rear view mirror,
pallid and monotonous life
that seems to simultaneously
race ahead
and lag behind,
yet leaves me standing still
looking for guarantees
of a trip worth taking.
Knowing full well life holds
no such promises,
I keep hands on the wheel
and head for home.

Pre-spring Malaise

Weak and apathetic
nothing feels right
even my favorite things
taunt with malicious intent

nowhere I want to go
nothing I want to be
except
alone
and even that's only a maybe

Don't want to inflict myself on friends
they deserve the very best
not this dull bovine creature
staring back from my mirror
spouting soporific nonsense
guaranteed to raise a yawn

spring is coming
time to be reborn
dress up my soul
in pastels
and hunt for leprechauns
and colored eggs

but oh I'm so tired
and full of the blahs
and I don't want to follow
the bunny building a hutch under my bed
I might find my track shoes
and have to join the race again

March 4

A Lifetime of Love

(Lady Lost in Shadows)

Her eyes flashed
and defiance shielded her doubts
on the day I proposed.
Marry someone without a history, she said —
someone young and untouched.
All I could say was I love you,
over and over again,
until her soft shell cracked
and she said yes.

We spent a lifetime holding hands,
with me saying I love you
over and over again —
when her eyes flashed defiance,
when bravado and my love
were her only armor
against a world with too much history
trying to repeat itself.

More than a lifetime ago,
I thought her spirit indomitable —
that nothing could dampen the fire in her eyes.
Until her steely gaze turned soft,
and I watched gray mirrors reflect empty rooms,
I never realized how much
you could miss someone
even when they're still there.

March 5

Hands tenderly stroke
head resting against my heart
Butterflies enter
The delicate dance begins
Float away on fragile wings

~ ~ ~ ~ ~

breezes whisper love
I bathe in their soft caress
wishing you were here

March 6

Like Love

Like love, spring snuck up on me;
one day when I wasn't looking,
the trees stretched bare arms to the sky
and the next thing I knew,
the world was amass of green,
rich and alive,
and smelling oh so sweet.
Like love, it filled my heart
near to bursting;
the sheer beauty of it
left me walking in circles
with this silly smile on my face.

March 7
Spiderweb Clouds & Angel Hair

I remember love
sifted through spiderweb clouds
and angel hair

Crystalline memories
ground more fine than
hourglass sand

A shimmering smile
crinkling your cheeks
and delight in your eyes

All for me
Tangible evidence
of your heart's desire

Nothing perfunctory
no counterfeit kisses

Alive in sensation
our love the most holy
and easy to follow doctrine

Flesh pressed to flesh
in sacred communion
blessed beyond redemption

Wrap me again
in spiderweb clouds
and angel hair

Create a new memory
to surpass all the others

March 8

For Susan

When I was five
my sister taught me songs she'd learned in school;
she sang in the glow of the night-light that she didn't need
to ward off the boogeyman hiding in the shadows.
I can still hear K-K-Katie and see
the peddler stroll the busy highway.

When I was eight
my sister taught me how to cross the street.
She wasn't supposed to take me that far
and I wasn't supposed to tell.
Being younger, but not wiser,
I let the cat out of the bag and
we both got in trouble.

When I was ten
my sister taught me how to iron a shirt:
do the collar first, line up the shoulder
to make a crisp seam down the sleeve,
and always save the body for last.
Useful knowledge I have passed along,
always remembering where I learned it.

For most of my life
I thought my sister didn't like me.
I was the baby, the little brat,
the pain in the neck she couldn't escape.
I just wanted to be with her — to be like her.

But we have always been different people.
Even as that gap narrowed with our maturity,
the bridge that joined us trembled with life's exhalations;
still we forged on, heads down against the wind.

In the end, those whose love created us
supplied the mortar to seal all breaches.
Echoed voices whisper, "Love your sister.
When we are gone, you'll only have each other."

My sister taught me people can change,
and that I was wrong when I thought she didn't love me.

March 9

The Dying of the Day

The day dies in flames,
a brilliant burst of orange and yellow
diving into the water —
I can almost hear the whispered hiss,
so contrary to the vibrant gloaming;
vivid colors enraged by the dying day,
silent screams voiced in chromatic splendor.

Death will not be denied
and still its lividity gives rise to a new dawn.

Faces

I see faces,
a sea of faces
in unlikely places:
in billowed clouds,
in the play of leaves in the wind,
profiles in ragged rock,
and patterns in tiled floors.
Sad or smiling,
sometimes forlorn or screaming
like the Munch painting,
trapped in a bit of mold
or a grilled cheese sandwich.

Unknown faces,
except for the time
when a charcoal sketched tiger
turned into Richard Nixon,
but I'd been using it as a focal point
through twenty hours of labor,
so I must have been delirious.

I have a photograph,
a shimmering white orb
floats over my shoulder.
Look closely and you'll see
a smiling face in the white;
I'm not imagining it —
others have seen it there too.
I like to think it's my mother's face,
that she was with me there
sharing my joy.

I wonder if all the faces I see
belong to people I don't know,
trapped in anonymity
till the end of time.

March 11

February Remembers

(for my mother, born February 6, 1919)

Through a window I watch snow fall,
fat flakes blown in the wind.
Warmed by the scent of hot chocolate
and thoughts of you,
I contemplate how long before
this sweet interlude ends
and it will be time to shovel the walk.

I remember the story
of your father's trek through a blizzard
to get the Italian midwife
who carried a gun for self-defense.
Tiny and perfect,
you arrived before they did.
You said it always snowed on your birthday —
or right around it.

There was no snow a fortnight ago,
but February remembers,
albeit belatedly.
Warm with memory I watch the snow
drip from the eaves like tears.
I remember too.

March 12

Escape

Escape loomed large in her dreams;
Leaving behind all life's irritations,
all the duties that called,
all the people who pulled at her incessantly
without care for her thoughts or feelings on the matter.

She woke to soft morning light filtered through blue curtains
and the neighbor's lawnmower vibrating in her ear —
or maybe it was her husband's stertorous snore.
It dawned on her that the children were grown with little need
    of her,
except as someone to vent their frustrations on
when life didn't go as they planned;
the job she hated might miss her hyper-productivity for a time,
but nobody was indispensable in the long term.
It might be time they all learned to live without her.

Wraith-like, she glided through her morning ablutions,
dressed and walked out the front door without notice.
Let everyone wonder... if they would.

Glorious blue skies kissed with lemon drop sunshine
and the sweet scent of springtime washed over her.
She stepped off the porch humming a happy tune.

The clock-radio shattered her brave new world
with news of traffic jams and terrorism.
She went to the kitchen and started the coffee.

March 13

Through Countless Millennium

I have looked at the moon thousands of times,
through hundreds of years and many lifetimes,
reflected on the water or casting shadows on green fields,
through a history of garments and sometimes none at all.
I have watched the moon cycle through time,
its wax and wane consistent in its inconstancy,
and know as surely as the new moon still exists in the
    darkness
that you and I have looked at the moon
thousands of times,
through hundreds of years,
and many lifetimes,
together.

March 14

Fairy Friend

Alone on the grass near the river bend,
a lad named Thomas stared up at the sky
dreaming of a world where he had a friend,
someone to listen, and he wondered why
he didn't. Suddenly a dragonfly
zoomed about his head; he tried to swat it
to no avail, too quickly did it flit
away. Then this dragonfly spoke, its voice
like tinkling bells, "Why do you try to hit
me? I'm just a fairy." I've no choice,

Thomas thought, but to believe it is true,
so he sat tall, and asked, "What is your name?"
"I'm called Torlan," she laughed, "What about you?"
With introductions done, they played a game
or three and soon a friendship they could claim.
"Will you come again?" Tom asked as sun set.
"Everyday," she said, "I will not forget.
Until winter comes, then away till spring
when first flowers bloom, on that you can bet."
Then she flew away on fast-beating wings.

Years passed by and their secret friendship grew;
true to her word, Torlan came every year.
Thomas grew to a man as boys will do
but never forgot the friend he held dear,
the one who was there through sorrow and fear.
Years flew by and Thomas saw loved ones pass
but always Torlan came, sweet little lass.
Till the day when Thomas, bent, old and gray,
met eternal sleep in the spring's new grass.
Sad, Torlan kissed his cheek and flew away.

16

March 15

London Remembered

(thoughts 10 years after)

City of palaces and parks,
green and blooming
flowers everywhere:
along walkways,
in window boxes
and hanging baskets.

Living history calls at every turn
from Speaker's Corner
to the halls of Parliament .
Ancient walls witness
the march of time,
surrounded by Tower tourists,
and unnoticed by the never-ending river of commuters,
preoccupied with iPods and cell phones
as they circle on their way to the Tube.

I imagined living in the shadow of St. Paul's
as I strolled along streets
where legends once trod,
and was awed.
As memory walks there once more,
I still am.

Avian Suicide

The middle of the afternoon;
the air is thick and still;
the sky a strange mix of dark and light
tricking fireflies into thinking
it is their time of day.
Thunder rumbles
louder and louder,
immersed in flashes of light
from God's own camera.
He blows out a breath
and comes a great wind;
eerie calm becomes wild fury.
I watch from a window
as trees lash and branches snap;
one branch lands in the front yard
trembling in the sudden downpour.

There is a bird standing not far away.
At first I am not sure
if my eyes are playing tricks
and that he is only a trapped leaf,
but then I see him dip his head
as if the giant puddles forming in my yard
are his personal bird bath.
How odd, I think,
as the bird stands so still,
except for the occasional bob of his head.

The air is alive and trembling
as the storm beats its way through.
Safe from my window
I will the bird to fly to safety,
and still it stands immobile
as the puddles grow deeper.
Guiltily I wonder if he's hurt,
but the storm is fierce,
and like the bird I do not move.

Maybe nature's birdbath surprised him
and fear turned him to stone.
Or maybe he decided the world is too cruel
and he'd had enough,
that it was better to drown in the rain
while my eyes capture the image
illuminated in the light of heaven's flash.

Called from my perch
I flutter to and fro
turning off lights and unplugging appliances.
When I return the bird is gone;
I am happy that he's decided
to give life another chance.
Storms always pass, after all.

Later when the sun is out
and I begin to gather
broken branches strewn across the lawn,
I find the bird where I last saw him,
his small body lying belly-up
with wings spread wide
in final surrender.

With a heavy heart,
I remember that little bird
who drowned in the rain.

The Eagles Mating

With talons locked,
the eagles spin and plummet;
seduction's dance is
their death-defying foreplay;
a public exhibition,
a dangerous preamble
to their private mating.

Screeching ecstasy,
overcome with potential,
they tumble through the sky,
forgetting everything
but the joy of joining.

Lost in passionate embrace
the fall from grace comes too fast;
the little death becomes the big one.

Eagles mate for life.
Dazed and alone,
without even an egg for company,
she mourns the loss of her soul.

March 18

Living Al Fresco

She takes her tea and cake al fresco
it's the only place left
where she can smoke in peace

Not like years ago
when she sat inside with the man
whose laughter made her heart dance

She studies faces in the crowd
ignoring the sneers of those
who think they know better

Was it so long ago
when they sat inside together
laughing in the corner booth

She sips her tea and savors yesterday
it's the only place left
where life tastes sweet

March 19

Love Abides

My mother chided me when I said I didn't believe,
"But you were so religious when you were a child!"
I tried to explain that just because I knew the theory
well enough to argue over answers in Sunday school,
it didn't mean I believed it was gospel.

My mother never argued in Sunday school;
she believed every word from the beginning
until her end. Sometimes I envy her that.

When I send up a prayer, it's to my mother.
Blasphemous to some, I'm sure,
but my mother never faltered in times of need,
her love and support were ever forthcoming.

Even now, when she's gone to her heavenly reward —
for surely there must be heaven for one who believed so
    fervently —
I feel her presence, watching over me,
offering comfort and courage when I need it most,
ethereal hugs wrapped in tangible signs.

I believe
Love abides.

March 20

Remembering Grandma

I can still see my grandmother's apartment,
so clear even though she's been gone
forty-five years and more.
A bedroom looked out onto the street,
a busy four lane avenue
that whizzed with traffic night and day.
Though she never slept there (Grandpa did)
there was a table loaded with plants in front of the window.
Lots of green split with the occasional flower;
I remember red and pink begonias
and the lilies they gave us in church at Easter most of all.

The kitchen was tiny,
and though my mother told me Grandma
could create miracle dishes with whatever was at hand
and baked blue ribbon pies no one could match,
I don't remember Grandma in the kitchen or baking any pies;
except maybe a pumpkin pie once,
but I never was a big fan of pumpkin pie.

Mostly, I remember her living room, which seems apt
because that's where she lived when she wasn't at the doctor's.
She had some rare spinal disease;
my mother said there were only ten people in the country who had
   it.
I don't remember the name,
only that she fought with the pain constantly.
I can still hear her moan, "Oh, my god," over and over,
which is strange because as far as I know she didn't believe in God.

When I was nine I baptized her—twice,
once with orange juice and once with water to make sure it took.
I was afraid she wouldn't go to heaven and I didn't want to spend
   eternity without her.

Strange how the world changes perceptions;
she didn't believe in God and I don't believe in heaven.

There was a twin bed in the narrow living room
that we shared when I spent the night.
We would stay up late watching Jack Paar on the small black and
    white television.
There was always a box of tissues and a glass of water
on a folding table beside the bed.
I remember the tissue Grandma always draped over the water,
to keep the dust out, she said.
There was a china cabinet too,
filled with pretty glass and trinkets she'd brought back from
    Bermuda
years before when she worked as a seamstress for Pan Am.
The hand-blown glass stirrers with tiny animal heads were my
    favorites.
I wonder where they are now.
Did they survive the years? Do they sparkle in some other curio
    cabinet
the way they still do in my memory?

All the shelves in Grandma's living room had plants on them.
Thinking back it's amazing that they flourished in a room with no
    windows.
Green. They were all green, no flowers there.
A green snake plant with shiny flat leaves
thrived in one of the green vases from Bermuda.
Even Grandma's green thumb couldn't convince it to take root in soil,
and her thumb was so green she once she even managed to grow
    gardenias in the bathtub —
which was quite a feat — at least that's what my mother told me.

My mother loved her, but my grandmother had not been as easy
    person to love.
It seemed that nobody liked Grandma very much—except me.
Nothing rivaled the time we spent together;
no better playmate or friend so true.
I loved her with all my heart, no matter what anyone else said.

And my grandmother loved me
with all the kindness, patience, and generosity she had never known
    as a child,
or been able to give to her husband or children or anyone else.
Her love took root in my child's heart;
her garden still grows there.

Karma

Before the moment of my birth
I was meant to love you.
Before managed time and calendars
ticking off the years,
you willed me to your side.
Spirits entwined on ethereal planes,
encompassing lives,
past, present, and future;
Einstein's theory proved fact,
existing everywhere and always —
together.

It matters not
if wisps in time
barriers separate us;
in the end
they will be bridged.
Angry words
and little deaths
are fleeting.
We are
forever.

March 22

Mosaic of Joy

Piecing together
a mosaic of joy
from shattered tiles
scattered around her,

she picks up
their first kiss
and declaration of love
and snugs them between
the light in his eyes at long ago reunions
and furious lovemaking on an ugly orange rug.

There are slabs
for the lives they created together,
the children who once quickened inside her,
who even grown have the ability to move her.

She fills in the cracks
with happy surprises
and hands held under pre-dawn stars,

certain that grout made from love
will last forever.

March 23

Blooms

A dozen red roses
wrapped in green paper and cellophane
tossed on a lawn.
Love, (lost or unrequited?)
left bleeding in the grass.

Around the corner
yellow daffodils bloom sunshine
at the side of the road;
a young man gathers
bouquets of spring.

March 24

Eating the Dictionary

She ate the dictionary,
swallowed the words whole
with no concern that she might become periphrastic;
words were a panacea when properly employed.

She marveled at words that sounded like their meanings
(beatific, diaphanous, zephyr, chimerical, ephemeral)
and more at words that didn't
(thaumaturgy, funambulism)
Sometimes she let them dissolve on the tongue, savoring
    their sweetness.

Some held a bitterness that made her choke
(rationalization, resignation, despondency)
and sent her searching for others more satisfying
(estimable, resolute, savvy, refulgent).

The more substantial words
(kindness, passion, intimacy)
always left her craving more.

March 25

So Close

So close
just a quiet thought away
that's where you are

now and forever

sweet sustenance
to nourish and succor

alone and hard pressed
I wish you were here
and then you are

so close
just a quiet thought away

touchstone for the rest

pitiable lot
who always fall short
of being you

With eyes closed
and heart open
you are so close

just a quiet thought away

March 26

Dreaming of Maui

volcano sunrise
splits the sky with bright color
cold dark flees in awe
above the clouds the world is new
and we are reborn with it

trade winds at sunset
palm trees hula in the breeze
sun dips into blue
drinking mai tais on the beach
life gets no better than this

dreams are temporal
paradise lasts forever
whisper I love you

March 27

Odd Memory

It's odd what I remember —
details of little things
like the brown plaid dress I wore on the first day of school
and the name of every teacher I ever had.

I can remember the date
of my favorite Beatle's birthday,
and the day that Neil Armstrong first stepped on the moon,

and the first time you said, "I love you."

I remember the way your eyes sparkled
and the joy in your smile
when I said I loved you too.

Yet I have retraced my steps three times
trying to remember why I went into the kitchen,
and I know there was something I wanted to tell you,
but now I've forgotten what it was —

maybe it was just "I love you."

March 28

Remember the first
kiss we shared, hot and wet,
lasting forever.
Winter's an eternity
when lips chap and turn to ice.

~~~~~

The bed springs creaking
a familiar pace, well worn,
like seasoned lovers.
Listening to the love sounds,
my body yearns for your touch.

35

March 29

I am whispered breath
softly inhaled
absorbed deep in your skin

The meaning of life
you cannot live without

Breathing velvet
chills down your spine
while flames burn within

Cocooned by ethereal kisses
gently blown on clouds
of hinted passion

We are one

Like unseen molecules
afloat in the air
the joining makes us
what we are

Breathe deep
I am there

Look to the Sky

I never notice
if the grass is greener
on the other side,
or even on my side for that matter.
It's all too close at hand
to be studied properly;
I find myself lost in the forest
looking for trees.
I search the sky
to find comfort and inspiration,
reflections of myself
lost in the black abyss,
sprinkled with diamonds
glittering in the night.
Hanging out with the man in the moon
or returning the slip of his Cheshire cat smile
I am inspired and consoled,
part of a greater universe
where I can only glimpse
the nearest corner
while dreaming of what lies beyond.
Azure morning skies
dressed in golden sunshine
and wind-blown clouds
beckon me to follow
more than any yellow brick road.
Dreams are born,
then flutter away
like homing pigeons,
to return on another day
when my heart is as gray
as the rest of the world
and needs a warming message
from a friend.

So if, by chance,
we walk together
down crowded streets
or a deserted beach,
don't be surprised
to suddenly find yourself alone.
I'll be back soon;
I'm only wandering through the sky.

March 31

Counting

I can't stop counting
the measure doesn't matter
three weeks or
twenty-one days
it's all the same
and time keeps ticking
backward

memories come uninvited
and stay for tea
while I recall in minute detail
the moments leading
to our last goodbye

tear-soaked whispers
of love and assurance
letting go when
all I really want
is to beg you to stay

inhaled breath
counting
long
seconds
until
your
final
exhalation

alone
I laid my head on your chest
knowing there were no heartbeats left
to count

I have done this before
days turn into weeks
weeks into months
months into years
always counting
backward
until one day
tears subside
and I begin to tally
the many joys
of having you in my life.

To The Point

Come to the point
where it is clear,
there is no point.
No more lamentations;
self-pity accomplishes
nothing of value.
There is no point,
only choices to be made,
whether to address change
or remain silent.
There is no point
in trying to change others;
we only have the power
to change ourselves.
We must delve deep, examine
who we are and what we want,
then decide how to make it happen or
There is no point.

April 2

Postcard to Heaven

Dear Mom and Dad,
Today is sunny and mild,
but spring is slow in coming this year.
Easter will be late.
It reminds me of childhood,
and shivering in new spring finery
we begged to wear
even though the season hadn't yet bloomed.
New hats and patent leather shoes
with a pocketbook to match,
white gloves with pearl buttons,
and ankle socks trimmed with lace.
I don't think that will be a problem this year.
Miss you both — wish you were here!
Love —

April 3
Without Me

I am nothing in the grand scheme of things.

Without me
there would be more chocolate
and even more brussel sprouts and asparagus.
Birthday and Christmas cards would not be sent
and gifts would not be bought and wrapped;
bills would not be paid on time and the checkbook would be left
    unbalanced.

Without me
the doctor said my grandmother would have died ten years sooner.
There are stories and verse that might never have been written.
There would be less laughter and
more tears shed with no one to dry them.
The beautiful human beings I brought into the world would not
    exist,
nor would their accomplishments or the joy they have spread.
There would be fewer hugs and kisses
and one less person to share random acts of kindness.

I am nothing in the grand scheme of things,
but the world is a little better because I am in it.

April 4

Doctors

Doctors are supposed to make you feel better
and I guess sometimes they do.
Certainly medicine has improved with time;
fewer people die of dysentery or strep throat,
and surgery is much easier for all parties concerned
now that anesthesia's been invented.
"Early detection" is their battle cry
to fight the "silent killers"
and cancers they've had some success with,
but they still haven't found a cure for the common cold.
Quacks still abound —
not every doctor graduated at the top of the class, after all,
and money is still the root of all evil.
Doctors are supposed to make you feel better
but they make me feel sick.

April 5

Monsters

Monsters
used to hide in
the closet or under
the bed when I was very small.
Scared,

I had
night lights burning
till dawn and my sister
calmed me with songs she learned in school
sometimes.

I still
remember them.
They're a sweet memory;
I wish we had shared more of them
back then.

We live
so far apart;
I see her so little
there's no time to create new ones,
alas,

Monsters
are everywhere.
Insidious, they creep
into my life—Who will sing to
me now?

April 6

Don't Just Sit There, Write Something

Don't just sit there, write something.
Pick up a pen and let the words flow
and spread over the page
like ink dropped in water.
Let one word lead to another
and another
and another
until you look up and wonder
where the time went.
Don't just sit there, write something.

April 7

Sadie's Song

What if my mother didn't die of influenza when I was still a girl?
What if Papa hadn't married a woman with daughters of her own,
who farmed me out as a seamstress, took my earnings for their
    fripperies,
and turned me into Cinderella without the happily ever after?
Maybe I wouldn't have run away from home
by marrying a man who loved me, but loved his drink more.
Maybe I would have known how to be a better mother,
one who, when her daughter came to her frightened by her first
    woman's blood,
had words of comfort instead of admonishments to stay away from
    the boys.
Maybe I wouldn't have learned to play favorites or been so cruel to
    the innocent.
Maybe I wouldn't have learned to desert my husband and children
with a man who said I deserved some happiness,
only to discover I must not have deserved it after all when he
    deserted me too.

Is kindness hereditary, carried on a recessive gene?
Is that why it skipped me — and all of my children, but one —
the unfavored daughter, so different from her siblings,
who took me in so many years later, when aged and in pain
I needed someone to take care of me again?
This child, who never really felt her mother's love,
loved me more than anyone else ever had.
Old lessons are difficult to unlearn and old habits die hard.
I could not undo what was done, nor wipe away years of too many
    tears shed,
nor show how much her love meant to me,
but I think she knew when I fell in love with the granddaughter,
who was so much like her mother.

48

April 8

The Wedding

The bride and groom walk
down the aisle over petals,
pink and white and sweet.
Happily ever after
promises exchanged today.

Friends and family
smile and dance, making merry.
Reach for the bouquet —
young girls battle for their turn,
wondering who will be next.

April 9
10:05 pm

My heart was pounding after the call came;
I raced to get tickets for the first flight the next morning,
praying you would hang on until I got there.
Twelve hours later I was in the air;
in another four I was by your side in the ICU
listening to your labored breathing,
grateful to find you breathing at all —
grateful when your eyes fluttered open —
grateful when you squeezed my hand
as you tried to say, "I love you."

For two days and two nights
I stayed by your side
with only brief escapes
to wash or eat or cry private tears.
I made small talk with strangers,
kind and well-meaning.
I said all the things I needed to say,
even the ones I didn't really mean:
that it was okay for you to go —
that I'd be all right without you.

I dozed in the chair
and awoke to the change in your breathing.
Whispering words of comfort (yours, not mine)
I waited as the space between breaths
dragged farther
and farther apart,
until the last
exhalation.
10:05 pm.
Two years,
one month,
and three days ago.
I still miss you so.

April 10
Never Again

I've been telling myself
"Never again"
for more years than I can
Remember.
Whether it's short
or long term memory loss,
I can't seem to
Remember
to
Never again
treat you the way I'd like to be treated,
because it's obvious that tastes differ
and you'd prefer
sarcasm, disdain, and condescension
to kindness, generosity, and courtesy.
Maybe it's not memory loss, but stupidity.
Whatever it is,
I wish I could hold on to anger and annoyance
like you do.
Perhaps then I might
Remember
when I swear,
"Never again!"

April 11

Maybe It's True

Maybe it's true and we've been together
before in at least three different lifetimes,
our souls linked by some strange cosmic tether.
That's what the tarot cards had to say. I'm
not one to argue, especially when
I'm unsure of the facts. But I believed
I had another life with laying hens
and animals we killed for food. I grieved
their loss and remembered other parents
than my own who I loved too, though not as
much. Perhaps I followed the army's tents
when you fought in some ancient war. It has
some merit, worthy of discourse, a view
you might consider and maybe it's true.

April 12

Winter's Been Long

Winter's been long and I'm waiting for spring.
I need the rush of new blooms gathering
to fill my spirit with color and light,
sweet hyacinth dressed in purple and white;
yellow forsythias make my heart sing.

I am renewed by signs of things growing;
this gift of nature tells me anything
is possible and everything's all right.
Winter's been long and I'm waiting for spring.

Fat bumble bees with pollen on their wing
flit to and fro with a buzz, zip and zing;
birds soar in the clouds to dance with a kite —
How I wish I could join with them in flight,
but I must see what tomorrow will bring.
Winter's been long and I'm waiting for spring.

April 13

The Music Store Clerk

Every payday, when she walked home from the bus stop
she'd turn into the music store she passed along the route.
Not a big chain, just a small local shop
where she could browse the aisles for new singles
with lyrics she loved or a beat she could dance to,
a zaftig young woman, alone in her room.

The clerk in the shop was a nice guy,
but not the stuff a young woman's fantasies are made of,
with dark curly hair that was just long enough
and eyes that laughed behind his horn-rimmed glasses.
Older than she was, but not so old that
he couldn't appreciate good rock and roll.

On a day when the store was mostly empty
he smiled at the young woman
who stepped up to pay for the new Rolling Stones record.
"You know," he said, "you have such a pretty face,
if you lost a little weight you'd be a knock out."
The young woman smiled and,
not knowing what else to do,
thanked him for the compliment.

As she walked the rest of the way home
she didn't know if she should be
more flattered or insulted.
Forty years later,
she still hasn't decided.

April 14

Mind Your Own Business

Pounding on the walls
voices screaming filthy words
mind your own business
shots fired—call 9-1-1
flashing lights arrive too late

April 15

Magical Thinking

Love is just another word for magic,
something science cannot explain,
though often biology and chemistry are involved.
There is no logic to it, no if p, then q
or formula to prove,
it just is.

Love is life fulfilled —
from mother's first love
to the hands of friendship clasped along the path,
to hearts joined to face the future,
whatever it may bring,
perhaps to begin the cycle over again.

Love is the reason
we fight our demons and diseases.
For at the end of days, what else is worth fighting for
except more time to love?

Love is feeling you smile in the middle of a kiss,
knowing it's all for me and always will be.
Love is just another word for magic.

April 16

Daddy's Home

Summer twilight,
children playing jump rope on the sidewalk
watched by mothers leaning out of apartment windows.
A little girl sits alone on the stoop, waiting
for her turn that never comes when the big kids play.
She stares down the street, waiting
for her father to come home from work.
Suddenly, he's there —
she sees him rising from the subway stairs
and runs to meet him.
His smile is wide when she throws herself into his arms.
Daddy's home!

April 17

A field of new cars
their rainbow colors gleaming
in the spring sunshine
wheeling and dealing bargains
tossing numbers scrambles brains

April 18

The Memory Keeper

I have nothing left but memories
to remind me of you.
No little trinkets you held dear;
no letters you wrote long ago,
no crocheted doilies or doll's clothes.
I cannot remember the sound of your voice —
there are no recordings of it —
I can only recall the moans of incessant pain.
The only tangible proof you ever existed
are a couple of black and white photographs
taken long before my memories begin.
I wonder how much of your face is true memory
and how much is drawn from those faded snapshots.
If someday dementia sneaks through my back door,
trying to steal all my yesterdays,
how will I keep you safe?
Where will you go when I can no longer
remember?

April 19

Love is Easy

Love is easy.
Like is hard.
Love is what keeps a parent
from strangling their teenager
when it seems they've been abducted by aliens,
who replaced them with obnoxious clones,
totally unlike the sweet baby they brought into the world.
Love is what keeps a couple
together when it's obvious
the honeymoon's been over for a very long time,
and strangers wonder why they're still together
when it seems all they do is complain about each other.
Love holds on when Like lies dormant
under the monotony of everyday,
waiting like spring bulbs to bloom again.
Love is constant; Like is flighty.
Like comes and goes
again and again.
Love is the blanket
that warms the empty places.
Love is easy and forever.
Like is hard.

April 20

Message in a Bottle

There is a quality to aloneness;
companions anchor us in time;
we are tethered by our communication,
both verbal and otherwise.
Without these connections
what we did yesterday or today,
or will do tomorrow,
holds no meaning.
I reach out the only way I can,
cast these words into the sea
with hope someone will find them.
You hold time in your hand now.
What will you do with it?

61

April 21

Second Thoughts

You asked about regrets —
did I have any and what would I change
if I could.
Sounds simple enough —
keep the good stuff,
toss the bad.
Trouble is
when it comes to regrets
there's not a lot of black and white;
mostly it's swirls of gray.

Good is often born of bad;
without pain there is no pleasure;
without ugliness there is no beauty.
To change one thing
we risk changing everything —
possibly losing what we hold most dear.
Actions have consequences.

Chances are
by eliminating angry words
or buckets of tears shed
over things that no longer matter
(if they ever did),
things might have been easier.
Or maybe not.
Maybe we would have dissolved
in indifference.

You asked about regrets —
did I have any and what would I change
if I could.
No, the risks are too great;
I have no regrets.

April 22

The Only One

You are
the only one
in the world who knows of
my most embarrassing moment.
You've kept
the secret
for many years
and I trust that you will
continue to hold fast that trust
until
the end.
You hold my heart
as I hold yours, always.
Together we are truly blessed,
Sweetheart.

April 23

Procrastination

Procrastination's a problem.
We keep putting things off —
things we should do,
things we need to do,
things we loathe doing,
which makes a kind of sense
I suppose.
Except we also put off
things we want to do and
things we enjoy doing,
which makes so sense at all.
I think
trouble getting started is
the root of procrastination,
because once we get moving
a feeling of accomplishment
often takes its place and
we're happy we've got it done.
I wonder
if we could figure out how to
motivate past getting started,
to begin someplace past the beginning
and start in full swing
Procrastination might not be a problem.
I'll have to ponder that
Tomorrow.

April 24

Prayer

What is prayer, but positive energy
set forth in the universe with hope that
good will come where it is needed most?
Does it really matter whether you believe
some deity is listening
or simply want to send whatever
love, kindness, courage and support
you have within to those in need?
What's in a name, after all?
Isn't the result what's important?
So when I say, "You are in my prayers,"
accept that I may not be depending on
a single glorious entity for results,
but on all the combined resources of the universe
to send what is in my heart.

April 25

The Nightmare

running
running
running
down a long
long
long
pier
shots fired
so many
shots fired
I am jolted
by the
impact
pain
oh the pain
I can see
the cool
blue water
ahead
there will be
no more pain
when I reach
the water
falling
falling
falling

April 26

Stormy Night

Dark and stormy night.
I follow the red tail lights
of the car ahead,
windshield wipers slapping time
with the pounding of my heart.

Strange man leads the way.
I wonder if he can see
better than I can.
If not, we may both end up
laying in a ditch somewhere.

Neon diner sign
ahead, welcomes travelers
with fresh, hot coffee.
Thanking unseen lucky stars
I run to warmth and safety.

April 27

In the Mirror of Your Eyes

In the mirror of your eyes
I am beautiful,
I am smart,
I can do no wrong,
and the world is a better place.
Like Narcissus
I wish I could gaze in that mirror
forever.

April 28

A World Without Sound

So much has changed
since he lost the world of sound.
Mostly he misses the music
that now he only hears in his head,
the laughter of children
and the sound of his wife's voice
when she loves him in the dark.
There are things he misses not at all —
the screeching of brakes
and chalk on a blackboard,
just to name a few.
Then there are the people
who think he's stupid because
he can't understand them,
and mostly he's glad that he can't
hear their slowly enunciated shouting.
But there are some things that haven't changed at all —
dandelion fluff drifting over a meadow,
shiny bubbles floating rainbows in the sunshine,
jellyfish dancing in the tank at the aquarium,
snow falling on a winter morning,
hourglass sand marking time,
holy smoke from church candles —
All this small silent motion,
so often gone unnoticed in the cacophony,
remind him
he is still
who he always was.

April 29

In the Thrift Shop Window

Attracted by a faceless mannequin
displayed in the thrift shop window,
the woman stops to peer through the glass
at the vintage dress patterned with gardenias.
She imagines its original owner — a society woman,
who accessorized with a wide-brimmed hat
and open-toed platform shoes.
Perhaps she wore it to high tea at the Savoy
or to watch her horse win the Grand-National.
She imagines the woman was a timeless beauty,
with graceful movements that turned heads when she walked by,
unlike the mannequin, stiff and forgettable in its faceless modernity.
She thinks about going into the shop to try on the dress,
but seeing her reflection in the polished glass
decides its loveliness really doesn't suit her.
She shakes her head and walks on.

Behind the Mirror

Behind the mirror lives a different reality,
a world of opposites from the one we inhabit;
a world where lost things are found,
where truth lies thick on the ground,
and the dead live reflected in the glass.

Once I tried to step through the mirror,
felt it waver around me like ripples in a standing pool,
felt your fingers reach out to touch mine,
but flesh and bone are too solid to pass through
and you were gone before we could make a connection.

www.ingramcontent.com/pod-product-compliance
Lightning Source LLC
Chambersburg PA
CBHW042129080426
42735CB00001B/12